Life Together in the United Methodist Connection

Life Together in the United Methodist Connection

Beth Galbreath

ISBNs
Print 978-0-88177-701-7
Mobi 978-0-88177-702-4
Epub 978-0-88177-703-1

Cover design by Joey McNair
Interior by PerfecType

At the time of publication all websites referenced in this book were valid. However, due to the fluid nature of the Internet some addresses may have changed, or the content may no longer be relevant.

The designation *UMH* refers to *The United Methodist Hymnal.* Copyright © 1989 The United Methodist Publishing House.

The designation *TFWS* refers to *The Faith We Sing*. Copyright © 2000 Abingdon.

Library of Congress Control Number: 2014930079

DR701

CONTENTS

PREFACE

Thoughts on Teaching and Learning

Each of us has a personal and unique learning style. It may be similar to that of others, but if we are able to use a learning style tailored to the way our brain recognizes, stores, and processes information, learning becomes easy and fun, and information is more effectively retained. Think of how you prefer to learn. Perhaps you are a reader. Maybe you learn more easily and efficiently by listening to music, to other sounds, or to voice. Perhaps you learn best in a "hands-on" manner. If the teaching method suits your learning style, you can process and adapt any information quickly. Addressing the educational needs of all students during a session may require you to modify your presentation style.

While lecture alone is the least effective means of presenting material, group activity is one of the most effective. Relational activities in small groups, or sometimes in the larger class context, associate students with different learning styles and thereby offer a way for the teacher to expose students to multiple avenues of learning. Although some sessions will lend themselves to one or more specific learning styles, the instructor can use a combination to address the needs of students. As teachers, we need to be creative!

Articles and guidelines concerning multiple intelligences refer to the research of Howard Gardner, or the "eight ways of learning." These disciplines can be loosely grouped into three categories or styles: auditory, visual, or tactile (also known as kinesthetic, as it can involve any form of participatory motion or perceived movement). Here are some activity suggestions:

Auditory
Class discussion
Show-and-tell
Creative rhythms and raps
Debate
Paraphrase or description
Music, songs, or rhymes
Poetry, storytelling, and reading
Word games
Seminars

Visual
Charts and graphs
Timelines and diagrams
Cartoons and bulletin boards
Photographs and video
Posters
Journal writing
Montages, collages, and collections

Tactile
Games and simulations
Puppets
Sculpting
Drama, dance, and role-playing
Singing
Construction
Experiments
Origami and jigsaw puzzles

INTRODUCTION

To the Course Leader

Thank you for leading *Life Together in the United Methodist Connection.* This class is required for lay servants who wish to become certified lay speakers. To earn a certificate for the class, participants must meet for five two-hour class sessions, in addition to worship at Lay Academy, preparation for the sessions, and reading assignments.

Learning goals are outlined at the beginning of each session. Sessions are designed in a way that enhance the learning goals.

Both the instructor and participants need a copy of *Polity, Practice and the Mission of The United Methodist Church* by Thomas Edward Frank (Abingdon, 2006) and *The Book of Discipline of The United Methodist Church* (current edition). In addition, the instructor needs a copy of *The Book of Resolutions of The United Methodist Church*, a laptop computer, projector, screen, Internet connection, whiteboard (or chalkboard or newsprint), maps of your jurisdiction (or central conference), annual conference, and districts, and copies of *The Faith We Sing* and *The United Methodist Hymnal.* Here is a list of needs that are session-specific:

Session 1: Provide notecards and markers for participants to make name cards so that their names are visible to everyone in the class.

Session 2: For this session you will need a picture of The United Methodist Church bishop's insignia, session 3 assignment slips to distribute (found in the appendix), and the chart of ordained, licensed, and lay ministry (http://www.gbhem.org/atf/cf/%7B0BCEF929-BDBA-4AA0-968F-D1986A8EEF80%7D/DOM_MinistryofAllChristiansChart.pdf).

Session 3: For this session you will need the Connectional Table diagram (www.umc.org/site/c.lwL4KnN1LtH/b.3897201/k.7965/Structure_and_Organization.htm), the document by GCFA titled, "The Financial Commitment of The United Methodist Church" (www.gcfa.org/sites/default/files/u3/Financial%20Commitment%20Book%202009-12.pdf), and a resource from your conference, if possible, interpreting conference apportionments.

Session 4: Include a YouTube clip for a humorous take on elections (http://www.youtube.com/watch?v=glouvidNcjg) and the jurisdictional map (http://www.umcgiving.org/atf/cf/%7Ba5da7032-3d61-4af7-88b9-96b0e1145ff4%7D/US%20MAP%20FM%20HANDBOOK.PDF). You will also need *The Book of Resolutions of The United Methodist Church* (several copies if they are available).

Session 5: For this session you will need the small-group topic assignments found in the appendix and several copies of the latest *Book of Discipline*.

United Methodist polity is a moving target and has the potential to change every four years. You will find that Frank's book is already somewhat outdated since it references *The Book of Discipline—2004*. It is important for you to help students learn to navigate the *Book of Discipline* and find the paragraphs to which Frank refers. You are urged to prepare carefully for the sessions so that you know what is coming.

If you are unfamiliar with what is variously called "the digital revolution" or "postmodern society" or "the Great Emergence" or "emergence Christianity," it will be helpful if you read either *The Great Emergence: How Christianity Is Changing and Why*, by Phyllis Tickle or *A Generous Orthodoxy*, by Brian McLaren.

There is overlap between this course and *Living Our United Methodist Beliefs*. Effort has been made to minimize the similarity between the two. While *Living Our United Methodist Beliefs* is not a prerequisite for this course, participants ideally have at least a general idea of the history of the Methodist movement. Frank's book covers this history and the historical development of our polity in detail, and you should familiarize yourself with the material though it is not part of the assigned reading for participants.

This course is organized around five two-hour sessions. If the format of your Lay Academy is different, adapt each session as needed, maintaining ten hours of classroom time. Each session offers suggestions for five-day and two-day Lay Academy structures. Sessions open with a short devotional that relates to the content of the session. The devotionals are also printed in the appendix to make them easier to reproduce and distribute to participants. The purpose of each devotional is to ground class instruction and discussion in scripture.

Invite participants to obtain Frank's book and begin reading it before the first session. Ideally participants will come to the first session having already read chapters 2 and 3. If your Lay Academy uses a two-day format, ask participants to read chapters 2, 3, 7 (pages 195-218), 8, and 10 in advance.

SESSION ONE

The Connectional Principle

Learning Goal

The goal for this session is to familiarize participants with the purpose of denominations, as well as the uniqueness, purpose, and overall structure of the United Methodist connectional system and its order of missionary preachers.

Welcome (5 minutes)

Welcome participants and invite them to give a brief introduction of themselves. Ask participants to use cardstock and markers to create large tent-style name cards so their name is visible to everyone in the class.

Devotion (5 minutes)

On the night in which Jesus gave himself up for us, he hosted a dinner for his closest friends. They came to the table and he washed their feet as a servant would. He said they should serve one another in the same way. He broke bread and shared wine with them. And then he prayed for them. Read John 17:11-12 and verses 20-23 aloud.

Then they left the table and went out into the world. Jesus knew that if they stayed connected with one another they would accomplish amazing acts for God's kingdom. But if they split up they would accomplish nothing and be lost from his fellowship.

When we celebrate the Lord's Supper we celebrate a sacrament of connection, a sacrament of unity with Christ and with one another. We come to the table with offerings of bread and wine to be consecrated. The bread of heaven is broken for us and the fruit of the vine is poured out, distributed, and shared. When we share in Christ's Body and Blood we are united, bound together, and connected with one another. At the table we receive spiritual nourishment for doing Christ's work in our world.

We are united, bound together, and connected in The United Methodist Church. We call ourselves a "connection." And we bring offerings of prayer, presence, financial and spiritual gifts, service, and witness to the church and world. When we come together at the meeting table—Administrative Board or Administrative Council, Annual Conference, General Conference, and the like—our gifts are consecrated to Christ's service, divided, and shared. Individually we might accomplish little, but connected and united we accomplish much for Christ's kingdom.

At this interval, invite participants to join you in singing one of the following hymns: *Bind Us Together* (*TFWS*, no. 2226), *Blest Be the Tie That Binds* (*UMH*, no. 557), *We Are the Church* (*UMH*, no. 558), *Jesus, United by Thy Grace* (*UMH*, no. 561), or *Blest Be the Dear Uniting Love* (*UMH*, no. 566).

Why denominations? (25 minutes)

Begin this section by summarizing chapter 2 of *Polity, Practice and Mission of The United Methodist Church: 2006*. Share with participants the idea that what we call The United Methodist Church

- is neither a church in the European sense of a national, tax-supported church to which citizens are expected to belong (such as the Church of England) nor in the Orthodox sense of an ethnic, national church to which all members of an ethnic group belong (such as the Russian Orthodox Church)
- is not a sect in the sense of a small, defensive minority within the boundaries of a national or ethnic church
- is not a mystical cult focused on one leader, although we appreciate and celebrate the influence of the Wesleys and Asbury, Albright, Otterbein, and Boehm
- is a completely *voluntary association* (Frank says, "Methodism was the quintessential American voluntary association, p. 67)

Ask the class *What do denominations do for us? What is their purpose?* Answers might include the following:

- training and ordaining clergy, and holding them accountable for their theology and behavior (church discipline)
- deploying (or providing a framework for deploying) clergy
- organizing and sending missions to evangelize and plant new congregations
- providing accountability for and efficient use of funds raised (church discipline)
- creating church institutions (hospitals, schools, charities)
- providing training and resources for members' ministries (such as Lay Academy)
- handling pension funds for clergy and lay employees
- continuing the theology and culture of the denomination through resources for practicing the faith—books, hymnals, liturgy, Sunday school materials, web resources, publications, and the like (church discipline)
- providing a sense of unity around shared mission, theology, and culture
- marketing (showing the community that the church is similar to others of its denomination in theology, practice, and culture)
- presenting an identity, a face to the wider culture, with hoped-for influence
- opportunities for assembly, inspiration, and fellowship (conferences)

The Connection Principle (25 minutes)

Begin this section by summarizing the principles found in chapter 3 of *Polity, Practice and Mission of The United Methodist Church: 2006*.

Now that we know what we expect our denomination to do, the next question is *How does it do it?* The United Methodist Church is organized differently from other large, voluntary organizations. The United Methodist Church has a constitution and the *Book of Discipline* that contain many organizational details. Would it surprise you to know that The United Methodist Church as a whole does not exist as a legal entity? Invite participants to open the *Book of Discipline* and look at the contents page. Turn to the Constitution and ¶139 which says that The United Methodist Church has no *legal* existence as a sue-able entity (Frank, p. 140). What then is The United Methodist Church? What "constitutes" the church?

The United Methodist Church is a *connection*. But a connection of what? People do not generally get together and incorporate a congregation and then come asking to join the annual conference. And annual conferences do not get together and decide to create a General Conference or The United Methodist Church.

Frank says that at its roots, the church is *an order of missionary preachers.* "Mr. Wesley's Connexion" consisted of all the preachers who were "in connexion" with him. He gathered them annually in conference for accountability, teaching, and assigning them to the circuits to which they would be sent. They were generally celibate, serving until they married and "settled." They agreed to go where they were sent, and Wesley agreed to send them.

After the American Revolution, preachers from the connection met in conference in Baltimore during Christmas 1784. They ordained Francis Asbury an elder in the church, and elected him to the office to which John Wesley had appointed him: superintendent (though he quickly began to be called "bishop").

It was the order of missionary preachers, meeting in conference, that constituted the Methodist Episcopal Church. The principle was the same in the Evangelical and United Brethren traditions. Today, ordained clergy (elders and deacons) continue to hold their membership exclusively in their annual conference. Bishops' membership is in the Council of Bishops.

The history of the next three hundred years is not part of this course. It is taken up in *Living Our United Methodist Beliefs.* Although much has happened in those years—laypeople now comprise half of all the members at annual conference—our church in a basic sense is still an order of missionary preachers covenanting together in conference.

Wesley's principle of "holy conferencing" pervades the church at every level:

- **Small groups**—the Wesleyan "classes" and "bands" making up the local society (now experiencing a renaissance)
- **Charge conference**—the congregation or congregations assigned to the "charge" of a preacher at the local level
- **Districts**—do not meet in conference but have important committee functions in screening candidates for ministry, encouraging and training laypeople, and the like (District Committee on Ministry and Lay Academy)
- **Annual conference**—at the geographic level; the locus of the preachers' covenant
- **Jurisdictional and central conferences**—at the regional or national level; the function of jurisdictional conferences in electing and

assigning bishops; they may do programming but only the Southeastern Jurisdiction does; the function of central conferences in making culturally appropriate changes to the *Discipline* for their context

- **General Conference**—the entire worldwide church

Small-Group Discussion (25 minutes)

Form small groups and discuss the following questions: *Why is our church organized the way it is? What are the benefits of layered organization and connection? What are the drawbacks?*

Class Discussion (15 minutes)

Reconvene the class and ask the groups to report on their discussion. Be sure the following points are covered under "benefits":

- The clergy appointment system, *itinerancy* avoids the expenses in time and money that "call" systems impose on local churches. (Also, if an appointment does not work out, the people can blame the cabinet instead of one another!) Moreover, the appointment system enables *sending* preachers to plant new churches.
- Clergy are thoroughly vetted before they are ordained, and if they become untrustworthy after their ordination, they are held accountable.
- Congregations with small membership can have pastoral leadership as well.
- Small-membership congregations can be part of a worldwide mission and ministry, and they can accomplish great things together that they could not accomplish separately.
- The conference provides services to local churches, including ________________ (Be sure you know your conference's services!)

Assignment (5 minutes)

See chart on next page.

Closing (15 minutes)

Spend time discussing the organization of your specific annual conference—its districts, district superintendents, the function of the superintendents, the bishop's cabinet, your conference boundaries and offices, your bishop (does your bishop preside over more than one conference?), and your jurisdiction or central conference. Be sure to have maps to use as visual aids. Ask participants to share what they know about each of these conferences. Do any of the participants serve on district or conference committees? Do they hold offices that must report at charge conference?

Five-day Lay Academy Structure Closing (10 minutes)	Two-day Lay Academy Structure Closing (10 minutes)
Despite the democratic conferencing principle, the United Methodist connection is an amalgam, a practical synthesis, of conferences and the episcopal principle, which we will take up next. Ask participants to read chapter 7, pages 195–218, and chapters 8 and 10 from *Polity, Practice and the Mission of The United Methodist Church* in preparation for the next session. Assure them that this is the longest assignment of the course. Ask for prayer concerns, and close with a prayer.	Allow more time for discussion of your conference's details and participants' service on local, district, or conference committees. Then say to the class, Despite the democratic conference principle, the United Methodist connection is an amalgam, a practical synthesis, of conferences and the episcopal principle, which we will discuss next.

SESSION TWO

The Episcopal Principle Itinerancy, Ministry, and Annual Conference

Learning Goal

At the end of this session participants will understand the uniqueness and purpose of the episcopacy, the itinerancy and appointment processes, ordering of ministry, and annual conference.

Welcome (5 minutes)

If this is a five-day Lay Academy, place participants' name cards where they were sitting in the previous session, or arrange them so that they sit next to someone different. If you are using a two-day format, you have five additional minutes for discussion.

Devotion (5 minutes)

If possible, have a picture of the bishop's insignia to show to the class.

On his last journey to Jerusalem, the apostle Paul wanted to meet with the leaders of the church at Ephesus, but he was in a hurry. So he stopped at the harbor of Miletus. Read Acts 20:17-32 aloud.

The church appoints shepherds—which is what the word *pastor* means—and chief shepherds, who are named bishops, for the work of overseeing the spiritual well-being and the ministries of God's people. Paul calls such leaders "overseers," and though the names and processes may have changed, his warning to "Keep watch over yourselves and over all the flock" still expresses the duty of bishops and their assistants, the district superintendents.

The symbol of the bishop is the *crosier,* (KRO-zher*),* a staff shaped like a shepherd's crook, symbolizing the responsibility of the bishop as chief shepherd of the flock of Christ's church. In The United Methodist Church, bishops are not a separate order of clergy. They are simply *consecrated* as bishops, not ordained, for the work of superintendency.

Bishops remain ordained elders among other elders, set aside, not as the *only* shepherds, but *leading* shepherds. The logo of the episcopacy in The United Methodist Church is shaped like a shield with a crosier running through it, and the symbols of Christ—the Chi Rho in the shape of the cross—and of the Father—the Alpha and Omega (Rev. 1:8)—are set against a red background, a symbol of the Holy Spirit.

Let us now pray the prayer contained in one of the ordination hymns, *God the Spirit, Guide and Guardian* (*UMH,* no. 648) or *Lord, You Give the Great Commission* (*UMH,* no. 584, verses 1, 2, and 4).

Episcopacy (20 minutes)

Ask participants the question, *What do we know about the episcopacy?*

In the discussion, be sure to cover the points listed below.

- United Methodist bishops in the United States have tenure for life (they are elected for terms in other countries), but they also remain elders. Their membership is in the Council of Bishops.
- A bishop's main power lies in the appointment of preachers. John Wesley (who was never called a bishop) and Francis Asbury had absolute power in appointing authority, and that authority, while assisted by the district superintendents, still remains today.
- Bishops ordain clergy, along with other bishops, district superintendents, and elders, all of whom lay hands on the ordinands.
- Bishops are *not* administrative CEOs of annual conferences, although they preside at conference sessions and exercise their appointive powers within annual conferences.
- Bishops are elected by jurisdictional conferences and assigned to their "areas" (one or more conferences) by the jurisdictional committee on episcopacy.

- Bishops have significant spiritual influence as preachers and teachers. The Council of Bishops has issued pastoral letters that do *not* speak for the church (only General Conference can do that) but urge consideration as an expression of their wisdom.
- The episcopacy is one of the principles that constitutes The United Methodist Church. After all, it was originally called "the Methodist Episcopal Church." Frank says, "The episcopacy is a constitutive principle of United Methodism by traditional practice, influence, and attributed authority far more than by organic law" (p. 127).

Spiritual Leadership of a Bishop (20 minutes)

Ask participants the following questions: *When has a bishop's leadership touched you spiritually? What is occuring in your conference that is empowered or enlivened by the bishop?* Be sure to keep the conversation a positive one.

The Appointment Process (10 minutes)

Outline the appointment process. If your conference's traditions—or your bishop's procedures—are different from what is outlined here, explain your conference's traditions or procedures instead. If you are a layperson teaching this course, you may wish to check with your pastor about how your conference approaches appointments.

- Each year at charge conference the church completes its church profile form. This gives the church the opportunity to say what is important to it in terms of pastoral leadership. The cabinet and the bishop take these forms seriously.
- Each year clergy persons also fill out a form indicating his or her availability for a move (this does not necessarily mean that the pastor or the church will get what they ask for).
- The district superintendents, who know the clergy better than the bishop, form the bishop's cabinet. (Bishops may also meet at times with an "extended cabinet" that includes other conference officers. But this meeting is not about appointments.) The bishop and the cabinet work together on appointments.
- Appointment changes may be initiated when any of the following events occur: a pastor retires or goes on sabbatical leave; a pastor

requests a move; a church requests a change; the cabinet feels a particular pastor is needed in a different appointment.

- The cabinet and bishop work prayerfully and seriously, trying to match the needs of churches, clergy, and their families. Eventually they agree to a particular move, and, usually, they plan a whole string of moves at the same meeting.
- The pastor's district superintendent calls him and (if the proposed move is to a different district) tells the pastor to wait for a call from the district superintendent of the other district.
- The district superintendent of the church where there is a vacancy calls the pastor and says something such as "We would like you to prayerfully consider a move to ______." This generally means "You are moving." A pastor can raise *serious* objections at this point, but they must be *serious* indeed.
- The district superintendent calls the staff-parish chair of the new church and sets a time to meet with the staff-parish relations committee, but without naming the new pastor.
- The district superintendent then meets with the pastor and the pastor's spouse to discuss the new appointment, followed by a meeting with the staff-parish committee. The district superintendent brings the pastor and the pastor's spouse to the committee to "*introduce your new pastor*." (The pastor is not a "candidate" or a "proposed" pastor.)
- If there are *serious* reasons that arise in the staff-parish meeting against the appointment, it *may* be reconsidered, but they must be *serious* indeed.
- If the pastor is going on sabbatical or retiring, his or her current church already knows about the change. Otherwise, the district superintendent calls the staff-parish chair of the pastor's current church with news of the move, which is not announced until worship the following Sunday. The grieving process begins.
- Simultaneously, the staff-parish chair of the new church announces the name of their new pastor, also not until the following Sunday.
- The district superintendent calls the next staff-parish chair and pastor in the chain, and so on.
- **Exceptions:** Founding pastors of megachurches may serve their entire ministries in the same charge. (Their successors will have quite a challenge, and they will probably serve short tenures.)

- If a pastor is moving from one conference to another, the bishop of the receiving conference must ask the bishop of the current conference to make the transfer, and the current conference bishop must agree.

Discussion (10 minutes)

Ask participants the question, *What is your general experience with the appointment process?* Avoid discussing personalities or specific appointments in recognizable terms. Guide the conversation toward the benefits of the process, and include the following points:

- Few churches go for extended periods without pastors, a common problem in a congregational call system.
- Smaller churches receive pastoral leadership one way or another.
- If a particular appointment turns out to be a bad match for the congregation, the people can blame the cabinet instead of one another, which shortens the healing process.
- If a pastor leaves for another church, it is usually not because the pastor was asked to leave, but because he or she was needed elsewhere. Again, there is no need to cast blame, and this shortens the natural grieving process that is always part of a move.
- Pastors with specific gifts and passions are matched with churches that need those particular gifts and passions for their mission.
- Itinerancy helps develop strong lay leadership.
- Itinerancy provides opportunities for women and persons from a variety of ethnic backgrounds to answer God's call, blessing the church with diversity and gifts that would otherwise be lost.

Emphasize that lay servants can help interpret the itinerancy system to their congregations, and assist them in avoiding the shock and anger that can occur when persons from other denominational backgrounds are suddenly faced with a pastoral change.

Ministry (15 minutes)

Summarize the main categories of our ordering of ministry. The terminology and structure of our ministry can be confusing. Invite questions and try to answer them. Participants are likely to be particularly interested in the certification of lay speakers and lay ministers. A chart is available from the General Board of Higher Education and Ministry at http://www.gbhem.org/atf/cf/%7B0BCEF929-BDBA-4AA0-968F-D1986A8EEF80%7D/DOM_MinistryofAllChristiansChart.pdf. You may wish to display this chart to the class.

Ordained Clergy

Elders—"traveling elders in full connection," ordained to the ministries of word, service, order, and sacrament; elders are pastors in charge, district superintendents, bishops, military chaplains, and involved in "extension ministries." Appointed by the bishop with security of appointment.

Deacons—also members of conference in full connection, ordained to ministries of word, service, compassion, and justice. Deacons are the UMC's *specialist* clergy: ministers of music, education, administrators, counselors, and an array of "appointments beyond the local church" (ABLC)—social workers, teachers, doctors, lawyers, principals, hospital administrators, community organizers, and chaplains. Deacons must find their own positions that are then approved and appointed by the bishop. Deacons have no security of appointment. Deacons who work outside the church also have a "secondary appointment" to a local church, but exactly what that means is determined at the local level. Deacons do not have sacramental authority (except in certain *extraordinary* situations approved by the bishop).

Licensed Clergy

Licensed local pastors—not members of conference in full connection. Licensed local pastors are counted as clergy and participate in the clergy session of annual conference. They are appointed by the bishop, but they do not have security of appointment. They have sacramental authority in their own charge only, an extension of the district superintendent's sacramental authority.

Lay Ministry

Baptism is the only ordination anyone needs for serving others in Christ's name. All baptized persons are called to use their spiritual gifts in ministry. Ordained and licensed ministry is rooted in baptism.

Certified personnel—both laypeople and clergy can take classes in one of many specialized ministry areas and become certified. As of 2012, certifications are available in camp/retreat ministry, children's ministry, Christian education, collegiate ministry, evangelism, ministry with the poor, ministry with persons with disabilities, music ministry, older adult ministry, spiritual formation, urban ministry, youth ministry, church business administration, and church communications. Certifications are available in undergraduate, paraprofessional, and professional categories.

Deaconnesses and home missioners—commissioned to lifelong full-time ministry of love, service, and justice. They are primarily social workers or involved in other helping professions. In some central conferences, deaconesses are primarily church musicians and educators.

Certified lay speakers—certified lay servants who have taken seven core classes: the *Basic Course*, *Preaching*, *Living Our United Methodist Beliefs*, *Life Together in the United Methodist Connection*, *Leading Worship*, *Leading Prayer*, and *Spiritual Gifts*. They serve in a variety of ways.

At this interval, pause and ask participants the following questions: *How do you use your lay servant training in ministry? How do you feel called to use it?*

Class leaders—The United Methodist Church is recovering the tradition of classes (small groups). Certification as a class leader is available.

Lay missioners—bivocational ("tentmaking") Hispanic persons who are appointed to start and lead new Hispanic congregations as part of the US National Hispanic Plan.

Certified lay ministers—A relatively new category of bivocational laypersons who serve as part of a ministry team in a congregation or lead a small congregation. Certified lay ministers are certified lay speakers with advanced training who also undergo screening through the District Committee on Ministry (DCOM), including all background and psychological checks, and are recommended and approved by the district superintendent and DCOM.

Annual Conference (25 minutes)

Summarize the points listed below. The United Methodist connection is organized into a set of conferences. It includes the following:

General Conference—the worldwide body that meets every four years and the only body that can speak for the church.

Jurisdictional conferences and **central conferences—**The primary function of jurisdictional conferences is to elect, appoint, and supervise bishops. They also set conference boundaries among other functions (see *Polity, Practice and the Mission of The United Methodist Church*, pages 270–272). The Southeastern Jurisdiction also runs programming, such as events at the Lake Junaluska conference center in North Carolina. Central conferences are national or regional conferences outside the United States. They elect bishops among other tasks, to which we will return later.

Annual conferences—This is the regional body to which your church belongs. Remind participants of the name of your conference, the number of churches contained within it, its districts, the name of its bishop, its offices, and where and when annual conference meets. The membership of annual conference is made up of clergy and laypeople elected from each pastoral "charge." The number of lay members of annual conference usually needs to be increased to balance the numbers of retired clergy (although many retirees no longer attend). How does your conference do this?

The annual conference does not exist between conferences, but it must provide for services to churches and clergy and also has staff and offices. Be prepared to discuss the following questions with participants:

- Who is in charge of arranging clergy moves so that individual churches do not have to be responsible for this?
- Who cares for clergy pension and health benefits?

- Who is responsible for print and electronic communications?
- Is there a conference media library that churches can use?
- What sort of committees, councils, and task groups exist in your conference?
- Who helps organize new congregations, site churches, care for property, and help local churches with building upgrades?
- Who mentors and recommends candidates for ordination on the district and conference levels?
- What other conference functions and committees exist? Mission trips? Conference mission agencies? Equitable salary support?

Charge conference—the local congregation is called a "charge" because the pastor is responsible for, or "charged with," its care. Once a year it will have a charge conference presided over by the district superintendent or another elder appointed by the DS. Special charge conferences may be called with the permission of the DS to approve real estate matters such as capital campaigns, purchases, and building projects.

Ask participants the following question: *On what district or conference committees or task groups do you serve?*

Each congregation's legally required committees (in the United States) are trustees, staff-parish, and nominations. Beyond these three committees, the local church can choose how to organize itself and what to name its teams, committees, and task groups. Each church will need a central administrative board or council to which the committees report and one that cares for keeping the wheels turning between charge conferences. Ask participants the following question: *How is your church organized?*

Assignment (5 minutes)

Prepare slips of paper listing general church boards and agencies, unofficial caucuses, and their special Sundays before this session. There are pages in the appendix that can be photocopied and cut into slips for this exercise. Choose the most important ones for your class so that each person will have no more than two slips. Place the slips face down on a table or fold and place them in a basket. Ask participants to select a slip(s) and research the group(s)/agency(ies) they draw. They will report on their research during the next session. Participants can begin their research by reading *Polity, Practice and the Mission of The United Methodist Church*, chapters 6 and 9 (pages 275–285).

Ask participants to include the group/agency's website in their report. If your Lay Academy is a two-day format and session 3 will occur the same day as session 2, adjust the sessions so that participants will report on their research the *next time* you meet.

Closing (5 minutes)

Share prayer requests and close in prayer.

SESSION THREE

Working Together Locally and Globally

Learning Goal

By the end of this session participants will have a better understanding of the many ways our connection works together to make disciples of Jesus Christ for the transformation of the world, from the local church to the global general agencies.

Welcome (5 minutes)

If this is a five-day Lay Academy, place participants' name cards where they were sitting in the previous session, or arrange them so that they sit next to someone different. If you are using a two-day format, you have five additional minutes for discussion.

Devotion (5 minutes)

Money is a part of life and also a part of the church. From the first moments of Jesus' ministry, he and his disciples possessed a common purse. Because they did not keep written records, they could not be sure that the money coming in matched the money going out. John tells us that Judas, the treasurer, found it too tempting and easy to skim from what Jesus and his disciples held in common. Read Acts 2:41-45 aloud.

Even when we do not live communally as the Jerusalem church did, *money connects.* Collecting and distributing money for the church's needs and for mission and ministry enables us to accomplish much more than we can do alone—and this in itself knits us together in connection. Read 1 Corinthians 16:1-4 aloud.

For Paul, this collection for the struggling mother church at Jerusalem was more than just money for a good cause. It was more than "apportionments." He knew that the *collection was connection.* Giving solidified his churches' desire to be part of the connection. And in the receiving, the Jerusalem church would confirm its acceptance of these Gentile brothers and sisters as equal parts of the connection of Christ's church. Paul did not take the collection alone. He brought with him emissaries of the churches in order to be sure that their offerings were given and received in full and the message of connecting fellowship taken home. Collection is connection. And money is mission and ministry.

Let us close this time of devotion by lifting our prayers through song (select one of the following hymns): *Rise Up, O Men [or "Ye saints"] of God* (*UMH*, no. 576), or *Lord, Whose Love Through Humble Service,* (*UMH*, no. 581).

The Connectional Table (10 minutes)

Invite participants to share information about the agencies and ethnic caucuses they researched for this session. Introduce this time of sharing with a brief overview of the Connectional Table (or whatever structure replaces it in 2016). Note that as of 2012, the efforts of General Conference to reorganize and streamline our general church structure was ruled unconstitutional by the Judicial Council. You may wish to share with the class this simple diagram of the Connectional Table: www.umc.org/site/c.lwL4KnN1LtH/b.3897201/k.7965/Structure_and_Organization.htm.

The purpose of the Connectional Table is to coordinate efforts among the general agencies. The link above explains the following:

> Leadership of the Connectional Table includes an Advisory Team with rotating membership coordinating the work between gatherings. Task groups, each responsible for an area of the Connectional Table's work, make sure the related objectives outlined by *The Book of Discipline* are accomplished. The task groups are also responsible for sharing information about the work in their particular areas with the entire Connectional Table for discussion at the semi-annual gatherings of the entire body. Such

organization has succeeded in distributing the work among the members and in moving forward the dialogue concerning vision and mission.

Student Reports (40 minutes)

With this overview and diagram displayed for participants, ask them to share two to three minutes of information about their assigned agencies, special Sundays, and/or ethnic caucuses. You may need additional time for this exercise, or less, depending on participants' brevity. Use a timer if needed. Here is a suggested order in which you can ask participants to report:

UMCOR
GBGM
GBOD
UMPH (and Cokesbury)
GCFA
UMCOM
UMW
UMM
GBHEM
GBOPHB
GBCS
GCORR
GCSRW
GCCUIC
GCAH
Ethnic Caucuses
Special Sundays

Apportionments (15 minutes)

Point out to participants that everything we have been studying is supported by the voluntary contributions of United Methodists. Share these figures from "The Financial Commitment of The United Methodist Church," a publication by the General Council on Finance and Administration: www.gcfa.org/sites/default/files/u3/Financial%20Commitment%20Book%202009-12.pdf. This is the 2012 edition. Use the most recent edition.

- Approximately 85 cents of every dollar in the collection plate stays in the local church.
- Another 12 cents goes to the annual conference and districts to support services to the local church and ministries of the district and conference.
- Just over two cents goes to general church apportionments.
- Almost one penny goes to other general funds and special offerings, including United Methodist Women.

- The general church budget passed at General Conference is divided—*apportioned*—to the annual conferences.
- The annual conference budget passed at annual conference is divided—*apportioned*—among its churches. (Some conferences still use the district Board of Stewards, in which apportionments first go to districts to be divided among churches. Find out and share how your conference does it.)
- The formulas for these apportionments attempt to take into account both membership numbers and economic strength of churches.
- There are seven funds in the general church apportionments:
  - World Service Fund—missionaries, overhead, and numerous ministries in the United States and worldwide
  - Ministerial Education Fund—for recruitment and education of pastors and bishops
  - Black College Fund—supports the historically African American Methodist colleges
  - Africa University Fund
  - Episcopal Fund—pays the salaries, office expenses, and benefits for bishops
  - General Administration Fund—overhead and support for financial controls, General Conference legislation, Judicial Council, records, and history
  - Interdenominational Cooperation Fund—supports involvement of the church in ecumenical organizations
- Annual conference apportionments support items in the annual conference budget. If possible, have a resource for participants about your conference's apportioned giving.

Apportionments are each church's share of the cost of participation in a worldwide connection and the glory of sharing in this worldwide ministry and mission. Note that the six special Sunday offerings support agencies and projects that are *not supported through apportionments*, such as UMCOR.

In addition to what is given through apportionments, the six special Sunday collections, the hundreds of Advance projects around the world, and dozens of partnership projects between conferences or individual churches offer unlimited opportunities for specific, targeted mission giving and involvement.

Charge Conference and Local Church Structure (35 minutes)

From the worldwide connection we now turn to the local church and its charge conference. You may review the point that the local church has wide latitude in how it organizes itself into committees and ministry teams. There is a church council to which the committees report. In the United States, the committees required by the *Discipline* are nominations and leadership development, finance, staff-parish relations (also known as pastor-parish relations), and trustees. Certain officers and members of certain committees are elected by the charge conference. Invite participants to turn to the paragraphs in the current edition of the *Discipline* that details the charge conference, church council, nominations and leadership development, finance, staff-parish, and trustees. The point is to familiarize participants with the location of these paragraphs in the *Discipline*, not to go over them in detail.

Discuss the following points. For each point, allow time for participants to ask questions, and try to keep the discussion positive. What are the reasons behind each principle? What are the benefits? (Paragraph numbers are from the *Book of Discipline—2008*.)

The local charge conference is ***part of the connection*** (¶¶256-251). A United Methodist church is not a "congregation" in the sense that a Presbyterian or a Lutheran or a Baptist church is an independent corporation.

- **The Trust Clause**—Church property itself is held "in trust" for the United Methodist connection. Property cannot be bought, sold, or substantially changed without the involvement of the district superintendent and the district site committee representing the conference (¶¶2501-2503). A local church cannot decide it would rather be Baptist or independent. The people can so decide and leave the church, but they cannot take their property with them. This principle dates back to John Wesley, and it ensures that property bought and paid for by Methodists remains Methodist.
- The local church **does not employ its pastors** (even though the IRS insists on churches providing W-2s for them, while also insisting that they are "self-employed" for self-employment tax). Rather, the pastor is a missionary appointed to a "preaching outpost" by the annual conference, and his or her "boss" is not the pastor-parish committee but the district superintendent. The pastor certainly pays attention to the annual evaluations of the pastor-parish committee, but only

the cabinet and the bishop can move pastors from one church to another. And only the clergy, meeting at annual conference and after due process, can "fire" a pastor from the connection. The differing expectations of pastor and people result not in "rules" but in a constant dance of working together (¶258.2 and ¶¶430–433).

- **The finance committee cannot direct how the church spends its money.** The finance committee's job is to help the church raise money to cover its ministry, which is determined by the church council (¶258.4).
- One important rule for financial accountability is that the **church treasurer** (the person who signs the checks) and the **financial secretary** (the person who receives and records donations) are ***not the same person***, nor are they members of the same family (¶258.4).
- **The trustees do not direct how the church building can be used.** They care for the building. The church council obviously has great influence on what ministries will be housed in the building, but ultimately it is the pastor's responsibility to see how the church building is used (¶2532).

Assignment (5 minutes)

Read chapter 9 (pages 268–275) and chapter 12 from *Polity, Practice and the Mission of The United Methodist Church.*

Closing (5 minutes)

Share prayer requests and close in prayer.

SESSION FOUR

Beyond Annual Conference

Learning Goal

By the end of this session, participants will have a better understanding of the connection beyond the borders of their annual conference—jurisdictions, General Conference, Judicial Council, and central conferences, as well as other international affiliated churches.

Welcome (5 minutes)

If this is a five-day Lay Academy, place participants' name cards where they were sitting in the previous session, or arrange them so that they sit next to someone different. If you are using a two-day format, you have five additional minutes for discussion.

Devotion (5 minutes)

Is church structure necessary? This is a tempting question to ask. Would it not be better to go back to the days of the early church and forget conferences and structures and councils and rules and laws? Well, let us return to those early days, and to the first General Conference—what the universal church calls the first Ecumenical Council or the Jerusalem Council referred to in Acts 15:1-29. Read this scripture passage aloud.

Conferences, the election of delegates, and the sending of missionary preachers, and even the passing of resolutions and the writing of minutes have been part of the church from the beginning. Let us lift our prayers for unity by singing the hymn of Charles Wesley that opens each Methodist conference, *And Are We Yet Alive?* (*UMH*, no. 553).

General Conference Elections (10 minutes)

When we think about General Conference, stomachs often churn. If you have audiovisual equipment available, lighten the moment by playing this two minute commentary from the Western North Carolina Conference on election of delegates for General and jurisdictional conferences: http://www.youtube.com/watch?v=glouvidNcjg. If your meeting space does not have Internet access, you can download the clip through www.cnet.com.

After showing the clip, point out to participants that what seems to be an error heightens the humor. With two valid ballots, the number required to elect is two, unless both were voting for Ken Carter. This humorous commentary highlights the confusion and frustration that members of annual conferences—and their bishops—often experience during the voting process. Highlight the following points and invite questions from participants:

- The most amazing aspect of General Conference is that it works at all, with six hundred to one thousand delegates speaking multiple languages.
- The General Conference secretary works out how many delegates each annual conference, missionary annual conference, or provisional annual conference may send by a formula based on the number of clergy and lay members of each conference.
- Once the number of clergy and lay delegates is established, separate ballots by clergy and laity are taken during the previous annual conference until the delegations, including several alternates, are elected.
- Balloting continues until an equal number of delegates are elected for jurisdictional conference only. All General Conference delegates are also jurisdictional conference delegates.
- General Conference worship can be richly inspiring and unifying; deliberations can be bitterly depressing and divisive. We will talk more about this tension in the next session.

Jurisdictional Conferences (20 minutes)

Show participants the map of United States jurisdictions found at http://www.umcgiving.org/atf/cf/%7Ba5da7032-3d61-4af7-88b996b0e1145ff4%7D/US%20MAP%20FM%20HANDBOOK.PDF.

Identify your annual conference and jurisdictional conference. Point out that jurisdictional conferences have the power to set conference boundaries, and that conferences have been consolidating over the last fifty years in order to save money. Is your conference the result of a merger? Are there reasons why a merger might be in your future? Ask participants, *What are the arguments for and against such a merger?* Review the historical reasons for why jurisdictions exist. Highlight the following points:

- The price of the 1939 reunification of the northern Methodist Episcopal Church and the Methodist Episcopal Church South (what now comprises the Southeastern Jurisdiction, roughly) was the segregation of African American churches into a Central Jurisdiction. The jurisdictional system ensured that no black bishop (or northern bishop) would ever be appointed to a southern annual conference.
- The deal was rejected in the Western Jurisdiction, which has always included its black churches and clergy in its regular geographical conferences. The Western Jurisdiction is the most diverse of our jurisdictions.
- Although the churches of the Central Jurisdiction were incorporated into the geographical jurisdictions and annual conferences in 1968, there are still two ethnic conferences: Rio Grande (Hispanic) and the Oklahoma Indian Missionary Conference. There is another missionary conference in the United States, Red Bird, that serves parts of Kentucky.
- All powers of the jurisdictional conferences are conferred by General Conference, as are the powers of the central conferences.

Central Conferences and Affiliated Churches (25 minutes)

There are seven central conferences of The United Methodist Church: Africa, West Africa, Congo, Central and Southern Europe, Northern Europe, Germany, and the Philippines. Participants may have heard of the Central Conference Pension Initiative, an effort to provide minimal pensions to pastors and surviving spouses in Africa and eastern Europe. Frank notes, "Central conferences have wide latitude to adapt United Methodist polity to indigenous cultures and practices . . . to manage church property according to local laws . . . They may adopt their own forms of rituals, ministerial preparation, or lay membership qualifications . . . [but] they may not enact legislation contrary to the Constitution . . . this results in constant tests of what is appropriate for cultural adaptation and what is necessary to remain part of one internationally constituted ecclesiastical body . . ." (p. 274).

If you have access to the Internet, give participants a taste of the diversity of The United Methodist Church by displaying the episcopal offices with their lists of conferences from www.umc.org (see links below). Or if some participants have access to the Internet on their cell phones, they can check these links out and share them in small groups and then report what they found to the whole group. The links listed below can be found under "International Churches" at www.umc.org.

Africa, West Africa, and Congo Central Conferences
www.umc.org/site/c.lwL4KnN1LtH/b.6572289/k.6198/Africa_Episcopal_Offices.htm

Central and Southern Europe, Northern Europe, and Germany
www.umc.org/site/c.lwL4KnN1LtH/b.6572295/k.7218/Europe_Episcopal_Offices.htm

Philippines Central Conference
www.umc.org/site/c.lwL4KnN1LtH/b.6572293/k.3BE8/Philippines_Episcopal_Offices.htm

Note the "provisional" annual conference designation. These are conferences that do not contain enough persons to stand on their own as annual conferences. In all these areas of the world, The United Methodist Church is growing fast, and it is now sending "missionaries" back to bless churches in the United States. Ask participants, *What immigrant pastors—or bishops—in your own conference do you know?* Highlight the following points:

- **Affiliated Autonomous Methodist Churches** and **Affiliated United Churches**: Some churches planted by US Methodists or others have chosen to be *independent* from The United Methodist Church but retain a covenant affiliation with it. Some churches planted by British Methodists are also affiliates. This category also includes churches that have *merged* with other denominations in their own lands, and the union churches still maintain an affiliate relationship with The United Methodist Church.

  These churches may send nonvoting delegates to General Conference depending on the agreement. Their bishops are not members of the Council of Bishops.

If your conference has a relationship with one or more of these churches, point this out. The "International Churches" page at www.umc.org also has links to these kinds of churches. If you have the time and technology, check out some of these churches, either together or in small groups. Point out any partnerships with your conference, and ask participants if they know of any such partnerships.

Africa
www.umc.org/site/c.lwL4KnN1LtH/b.6136173/k.7244/Affiliated_Churches__Africa.htm

Asia
www.umc.org/site/c.lwL4KnN1LtH/b.6136171/k.4C90/Affiliated_Churches__Asia.htm

Central America/Caribbean
www.umc.org/site/c.lwL4KnN1LtH/b.6136177/k.28F/Affiliated_Churches__Central_AmericaCaribbean.htm

Europe
www.umc.org/site/c.lwL4KnN1LtH/b.6136167/k.7668/Affiliated_Churches__Europe.htm

South America
www.umc.org/site/c.lwL4KnN1LtH/b.6136181/k.1CA9/Affiliated_Churches__South_America.htm

- **Nonaffiliated Autonomous and United Churches**: Conferences and churches and the General Board of Global Ministries may also have partnerships with churches of the Methodist tradition that do not have formal agreements or relationships with The United Methodist Church, such as the Church of South India (a union church) and the Methodist Church of Haiti, both of which are not listed as affiliated.

  Invite participants to look at the "Members A to Z" list on the World Methodist Council website and observe the diversity of the descendents of John Wesley: http://worldmethodistcouncil.org/about/member-churches-a-to-z.

Judicial Council (20 minutes)

Highlight the following points from chapter 12 of *Polity, Practice and the Mission of The United Methodist Church*:

- The Judicial Council has nine members, five laity and four clergy in one quadrennium and five clergy and four laity in the next. They serve eight-year terms and may be reelected. The council elects its own officers and sets its own rules.
- Members are nominated by the Council of Bishops, which names three times the number of persons needed to fill the vacancies. General Conference then elects the council from this slate.
- Decisions made by the Judicial Council include:
    - declaratory judgments about the constitutionality or legality of actions taken by any body in the connection
    - automatic review of legal decisions by bishops presiding over conferences
    - appeals of bishops' decisions of law which are submitted by a fifth of the annual conference's members
    - appeals of legal questions that arise from church trials and similar actions

  Although we will not go into detail, the 2012 General Conference struggled with efforts to rearrange the church's administrative structure only to have their efforts fail or be declared unconstitutional by the Judicial Council.

The Book of Resolutions (10 minutes)

Because only General Conference can speak for The United Methodist Church, General Conference deals with thousands of resolutions. If you have copies of the *Book of Resolutions,* share them with participants so they can see the variety of subjects it addresses. Emphasize the point that these resolutions are the best efforts of the delegates to faithfully address issues of concern to the world. Sometimes the resolutions may contradict one another (even in the same paragraph) and they are not church law. Frank says, "The General Conference asks all United Methodists to consider these positions and accept them as the collective wisdom of the church, but it does not expect all United Methodists to agree with such statements" (p. 264).

Discussion (15 minutes)

Ask participants the following questions: *What is new or surprising to you? What inspires you? If you were in charge, is there anything that you would change?*

Below is a quote by Reverend Christy Thomas of Krum First United Methodist Church in Krum, Texas, published in the United Methodist Reporter in November 2012. If time allows, read the quote aloud and discuss it with the class. If time does not allow you to read aloud and discuss it at this interval, read it at the end of the session, and ask participants to think about it as they read the assignment and consider the tensions in the structure of The United Methodist Church in preparation for the next session.

> The United Methodist Church cannot be re-formed. It's over for us with our current structure . . . It's easy to get frustrated with the Judicial Council for the rulings of the last few months. Their work has thoroughly reversed decisions made by General and Jurisdictional Conferences. . . . Because the members of the Council were faithful to the letter of the law, which is exactly what they are supposed to do, we now know for sure that this emperor has no clothes . . . [substantial and necessary change under the current rules] can't work. Period.
>
> We are going to have to engender our own revolution/reformation or die slowly of strangulation by methods that no longer support the heart of Methodism. . . .
>
> We have the most powerful theology of grace that has ever infused the human race. . . . Can grace-infused theology hold us together in the revolution that is now necessary? Can we plant ourselves firmly on opposite sides of huge issues, pray, argue and fight our way through this, and see a healthy and actually united Methodist church born yet once more? Can we free ourselves from the death strangle of our current methods and still be Methodists?

After reading the quote ask participants, *Do you agree with what Reverend Thomas says here? Why or why not?*

Assignment (5 minutes)

Read chapter 7 in *Polity, Practice and the Mission of The United Methodist Church* (pages 218–229) and the conclusion. Note: You may wish to assign the opening devotion for the next session to two or more participants who may want to share the reading. Also, in your own planning for the next session, consider what issues and concerns seem to be most important to participants.

Closing (5 minutes)

Share prayer requests and close in prayer.

SESSION FIVE

For Such a Time as This

Learning Goal

In this session participants will consider two aspects of our life together as United Methodists using various formats for discussion and conferencing. This session will equip participants with new insights and tools for discernment in making decisions in their local church and—perhaps—their conference.

Welcome (5 minutes)

If this is a five-day Lay Academy, place participants' name cards where they were sitting in the previous session, or arrange them so that they sit next to someone different. If you are using a two-day format, you have five additional minutes for discussion.

Devotion (5 minutes)

In the book of Esther, Mordecai asks his ward, Queen Esther, to risk her life and challenge the decree of destruction that has been issued against the Jews in Persia. Mordecai says, "Do not think that in the king's palace you will escape any more than all the other Jews. . . . Who knows? Perhaps you have come to royal dignity for just such a time as this" (Esther 4:13-14).

We are living in a time of deep turmoil, tremendous challenge, and significant change. Perhaps as lay servants we have been called to this ministry in our beloved United Methodist Church for such a time as this. It is a time much like another time of turmoil, challenge, and change, in which Jesus taught. . . Read Matthew 5:1-14 aloud, pausing after each beatitude.

Often the wrangling that occurs in our churches and conferences dims God's light and fails to give God glory. Sometimes we finite human beings must admit in all humility that we cannot be entirely sure *what* gives God glory in a given situation. As Paul notes, there will be disagreements in the church and the church must work its way through them and move toward the truth of God's call in such a time as this.

Can we learn to disagree with love and grace, with humility, meekness, hunger for righteousness, mercy, purity, and peacemaking? Can God be glorified even in our conflicts? Let us pray that God may be so glorified as we sing (select one of the following hymns): *Christ Has Risen* (*TFWS*, no. 2115), *Lord, Be Glorified* (*TFWS*, no. 2150), *I'm Gonna Live So God Can Use Me* (*TFWS*, no. 2153), *Let There Be Peace on Earth* (*UMH*, no. 431).

Such a Time as This (15 minutes)

Summarize the changes in world culture during the early twenty-first century from your own perspective or that of Phyllis Tickle or Brian McLaren. Do not dwell on the negative. Be sure to highlight the following points:

- the change in a system of communication that was *primarily* print-based to *primarily* digital-based, which has wrenching implications for every culture in the world, including how we work, how we worship, how we think, and even our attention spans
- the demographic shift of the center of Christianity to the southern hemisphere, and the demographic shift of the center of The United Methodist Church to Africa and Asia
- the consumer attitude of persons in the United States who attend church, in which shopping for a church that meets their family's needs is more important than denominational loyalty or theology
- the deep suspicion of (or disappointment in?) "organized religion" and the rise of secular and para-church organizations engaging in much of the mission and ministry that was once the province of the denominations: Oxfam, CARE, Heifer Project, Habitat for Humanity, Church World Service, Doctors Without Borders, the Gates Foundation, and thousands of local charities specific in purpose and

government programs—food pantries, homeless shelters, free clinics, park district programs, and the like
- the rising challenge to authority, particularly religious authority and hierarchy, as knowledge and authority become democratized or "crowdsourced"
- the rising interest in the work of the Holy Spirit throughout the church, giving rise to charismatic and Pentecostal movements worldwide as well as renewed efforts in spiritual formation in mainline denominations (Upper Room, Walk to Emmaus, Academy for Spiritual Formation, spiritual direction, covenant groups, Taizé music and worship)
- "Ancient-future" church, meaning renewed interest in deeply meaningful celebration of the sacraments of Communion and baptism, and other physical acts and sensory elements in worship, such as candles, incense, fountains, footwashing, reaffirmation of baptism, labyrinths, and the like
- the challenges of the digital age—what parts of worship are appropriate to post online? Some churches now stream their worship services online, and other congregations exist *only* online (how do we care for all the dimensions of discipleship—sacraments, small-group interaction, and service—in our digital age?)
- the challenges of increasing diversity as our children marry across racial and religious lines, change denominations or convert to other faiths, or are more open about sexual orientation

What does this mean for the church? It is the reality of our time and the background against which the polity of The United Methodist Church must either work or change.

Small-Group Discussion I (30 minutes)

For the remainder of the session, invite participants to form small groups of three or four persons each. Participants will receive a challenge assignment in an attempt to use what they have learned in the course to guide their discussion. Assign a facilitator in each group to read the assignment. Each group should then choose a person to serve as the reporter who will report their group's discussion to the entire class. The challenge assignments can be found in the appendix.

Class Discussion (15 minutes)

Ask the reporter in each group to report on their group's discussion by answering the following questions: *What issue was your group assigned? What, if anything, does the Discipline say about the issue? Did everyone in the group have a chance to participate in the discussion? When in the discussion was Christian love shown?*

Distribute the second assignment to the small groups. If you wish, you may rearrange the groups for the second small-group discussion in order to add variety to the exercise.

Small-Group Discussion II (30 minutes)

Follow the same pattern as Small-Group Discussion I. If some groups finish before the fifteen minutes allotted for this exercise is over, you may assign a third discussion to those groups.

Class Discussion (15 minutes)

Ask the reporter in each group to report on their group's discussion by answering the following questions: *What issue was your group assigned? What, if anything, does the Discipline say about the issue? Did everyone in the group have a chance to participate in the discussion? When in the discussion was Christian love shown?*

Closing (5 minutes)

Allow the closing to be a time for participants to recenter themselves, if necessary, after the intensity of the small-groups discussions, and then lead participants in the closing devotion. Invite participants to read the quotes below, one by the Reverend Christy Thomas, a contemporary pastor, and the other by John Wesley.

Reverend Thomas asks, "Can we free ourselves from the death strangle of our current methods and still be Methodists?" She answers the question by saying, "If we can't, or we won't, then we need to die anyway. We deserve no better than to slowly lose oxygen as we wander forever lost through the dead-end maze known as the *Book of Discipline*. If we can and we will, then we will unleash the Spirit of God yet once more. It's time" (http://christythomas.com/?s=strangulation).

In sermon 39, "Catholic Spirit," John Wesley lifts up several of the scriptural comments on the Great Commandment. He writes:

> [Jesus said,] "A new commandment I give unto you, That ye love one another: as I have loved you, that ye also love one another. By this shall all men know that ye are My disciples, if ye have love one to another. . . ." This is that love on which the Apostle John so frequently and strongly insists. . . . "Not that we loved God, but that he loved us, and sent his Son to be the propitiation for our sins. Beloved, if God so loved us, we ought also to love one another. . . ."
>
> All men approve of this; but do all men practise it? Daily experience shows the contrary. Where are even the Christians who "love one another as he hath given us commandment?" How many hindrances lie in the way! The two grand, general hindrances are, first, that they cannot all think alike and, in consequence of this, secondly, they cannot all walk alike; but in several smaller points their practice must differ in proportion to the difference of their sentiments. . . .
>
> But although a difference in opinions or modes of worship may prevent an entire external union, yet need it prevent our union in affection? Though we cannot think alike, may we not love alike? May we not be of one heart, though we are not of one opinion? Without all doubt, we may. Herein all the children of God may unite, notwithstanding these smaller differences. These remaining as they are, they may forward one another in love and in good works (www.ccel.org/ccel/wesley/sermons.pdf).

As twenty-first-century Methodists, we need to renew our connection in ways that will, as our founder, John Wesley, said it, "forward one another in love and in good works" even though we do not all think alike or worship alike or walk alike. We need the Holy Spirit's help to renew our life together.

Invite participants to spend time in silent prayer. You may then close by offering a prayer of your own or by singing *They'll Know We Are Christians by Our Love* (*TFWS*, no. 2223).

Appendix

Devotion for Session One

On the night in which Jesus gave himself up for us, he hosted a dinner for his closest friends. They came to the table and he washed their feet as a servant would. He said they should serve one another in the same way. He broke bread and shared wine with them. And then he prayed for them. Read John 17:11-12 and verses 20-23 aloud.

Then they left the table and went out into the world. Jesus knew that if they stayed connected with one another they would accomplish amazing acts for God's kingdom. But if they split up they would accomplish nothing and be lost from his fellowship.

When we celebrate the Lord's Supper we celebrate a sacrament of connection, a sacrament of unity with Christ and with one another. We come to the table with offerings of bread and wine to be consecrated. The bread of heaven is broken for us and the fruit of the vine is poured out, distributed, and shared. When we share in Christ's Body and Blood we are united, bound together, and connected with one another. At the table we receive spiritual nourishment for doing Christ's work in our world.

We are united, bound together, and connected in The United Methodist Church. We call ourselves a *connection.* And we bring offerings of prayers, presence, financial and spiritual gifts, service, and witness to the church and world. When we come together at the meeting table—Administrative Board or Administrative Council, Annual Conference, General Conference, and the like—our gifts are consecrated to Christ's service, divided, and shared. Individually we might accomplish little, but connected and united, we accomplish much for Christ's kingdom.

At this interval, invite participants to join you in singing one of the following hymns: *Bind Us Together* (*TFWS*, no. 2226), *Blest Be the Tie That Binds* (*UMH*, no. 557), *We Are the Church* (*UMH*, no. 558), *Jesus, United by Thy Grace* (*UMH*, no. 561), or *Blest Be the Dear Uniting Love* (*UMH*, no. 566).

Devotion for Session Two

If possible, have a picture of the bishop's insignia to show to the class.

On his last journey to Jerusalem, the apostle Paul wanted to meet with the leaders of the church at Ephesus, but he was in a hurry. So he stopped at the harbor of Miletus. Read Acts 20:17-32 aloud.

The church appoints shepherds—which is what the word *pastor* means—and chief shepherds, who are named bishops, for the work of overseeing the spiritual well-being and the ministries of God's people. Paul calls such leaders "overseers," and though the names and processes may have changed, his warning to "Keep watch over yourselves and over all the flock" still expresses the duty of bishops and their assistants, the district superintendents.

The symbol of the bishop is the *crosier,* (KRO-zher*),* a staff shaped like a shepherd's crook, symbolizing the responsibility of the bishop as chief shepherd of the flock of Christ's church. In The United Methodist Church, bishops are not a separate order of clergy. They are simply *consecrated* as bishops, not ordained, for the work of superintendency.

Bishops remain ordained elders among other elders, set aside, not as the *only* shepherds, but *leading* shepherds. The logo of the episcopacy in The United Methodist Church is shaped like a shield with a crosier running through it, and the symbols of Christ—the Chi Rho in the shape of the cross—and of the Father—the Alpha and Omega (Rev. 1:8)—are set against a red background, a symbol of the Holy Spirit.

Let us now pray the prayer contained in one of the ordination hymns, *God the Spirit, Guide and Guardian* (*UMH*, no. 648) or *Lord, You Give the Great Commission* (*UMH*, no. 584, verses 1, 2, and 4).

Devotion for Session Three

Money is a part of life and also a part of the church. From the first moments of Jesus' ministry, he and his disciples possessed a common purse. Because they did not keep written records, they could not be sure that the money coming in matched the money going out. John tells us that Judas, the treasurer, found it too tempting and easy to skim from what Jesus and his disciples held in common. Read Acts 2:41-45 aloud.

Even when we do not live communally as the Jerusalem church did, *money connects.* Collecting and distributing money for the church's needs and for mission and ministry enable us to accomplish much more than we can do alone—and this in itself knits us together in connection. Read 1 Corinthians 16:1-4 aloud.

For Paul, this collection for the struggling mother church at Jerusalem was more than just money for a good cause. It was more than "apportionments." He knew that the *collection was connection.* Giving solidified his churches' desire to be part of the connection. And in the receiving, the Jerusalem church would confirm its acceptance of these Gentile brothers and sisters as equal parts of the connection of Christ's church. Paul did not take the collection alone. He brought with him emissaries of the churches in order to be sure that their offerings were given and received in full and the message of connecting fellowship taken home. Collection is connection. And money is mission and ministry.

Let us close this time of devotion by lifting our prayers through song (select one of the following hymns): *Rise Up, O Men [or "Ye saints"] of God* (*UMH,* no. 576), or *Lord, Whose Love Through Humble Service,* (*UMH,* no. 581).

Devotion for Session Four

Is church structure necessary? This is a tempting question to ask. Would it not be better to go back to the days of the early church and forget conferences and structures and councils and rules and laws? Well, let us return to those early days, and to the first General Conference—what the universal church calls the first Ecumenical Council or the Jerusalem Council referred to in Acts 15:1-29. Read the scripture passage aloud.

Conferences, the election of delegates, and the sending of missionary preachers, and even the passing of resolutions and the writing of minutes have been part of the church from the beginning. Let us lift our prayers for unity by singing the hymn of Charles Wesley that opens each Methodist conference, *And Are We Yet Alive?* (*UMH*, no. 553).

Devotion for Session Five

In the book of Esther, Mordecai asks his ward, Queen Esther, to risk her life and challenge the decree of destruction that has been issued against the Jews in Persia. Mordecai says, "Do not think that in the king's palace you will escape any more than all the other Jews. . . . Who knows? Perhaps you have come to royal dignity for just such a time as this" (Esther 4:13-14).

We are living in a time of deep turmoil, tremendous challenge, and significant change. Perhaps as lay servants we have been called to this ministry in our beloved United Methodist Church for such a time as this. It is a time much like another time of turmoil, challenge, and change, in which Jesus taught. . . Read Matthew 5:1-14 aloud, pausing after each beatitude.

Often the wrangling that occurs in our churches and conferences dims God's light and fails to give God glory. Sometimes we finite human beings must admit in all humility that we cannot be entirely sure *what* gives God glory in a given situation. As Paul notes, there will be disagreements in the church and the church must work its way through them and move toward the truth of God's call in such a time as this.

Can we learn to disagree with love and grace, with humility, meekness, hunger for righteousness, mercy, purity, and peacemaking? Can God be glorified even in our conflicts? Let us pray that God may be so glorified as we sing (select one of the following hymns): *Christ Has Risen* (*TFWS*, no. 2115), *Lord, Be Glorified* (*TFWS*, no. 2150), *I'm Gonna Live So God Can Use Me* (*TFWS*, no. 2153), *Let There Be Peace on Earth* (*UMH*, no. 431).

Letter to the Course Participant

Welcome to this Lay Servant Ministries class on the polity of The United Methodist Church. This course is based on the book *Polity, Practice and the Mission of The United Methodist Church*, by Thomas Edward Frank.

Polity is a word that may sound both scary and boring. Scary because we may associate the word with *politics,* and boring because we may also associate it with terms like *meeting* and *Book of Discipline* and *law* and *legality*. But the word *polity* in this context simply refers to the way in which we organize ourselves as United Methodists and live and work together. In The United Methodist Church, we have a deep understanding of the *purpose* of the way we organize ourselves—a deep understanding of the *holiness* of living together to build one another up, and working together to do the work that we as the body of Christ are called to do.

In this course, we will explore some of the biblical roots of the church and how we as United Methodists organize ourselves to live together and do the work we are called to do. We will see how administrative meetings can serve as both channels of God's grace and a means for each of us to employ our spiritual gifts in God's service. We will also begin preparing ourselves for the challenging and exciting times that lie ahead for the people called United Methodist in the twenty-first century.

If you are participating in this class as part of a Lay Academy, you will meet for a total of ten hours. Lay Academy events include opening and closing worship and lunch. You will enjoy this class more if you obtain the textbook ahead of time and begin reading it.

There are two books you will need for this class: *Polity, Practice and the Mission of The United Methodist Church,* by Thomas Edward Frank, published by Abingdon, and *The Book of Discipline of The United Methodist Church* (current edition).

Welcome to *Life Together in the United Methodist Connection*!

Session 3 Assignment slips

(Note: Distribute these to participants at the end of session 2).

General Commission on Archives & History
The United Methodist Church

www.gcah.org

United Methodist
communications

www.umcom.org

GENERAL COMMISSION ON CHRISTIAN UNITY AND INTERRELIGIOUS CONCERNS *The United Methodist Church*

www.gccuic-umc.org

What does the website say about ecumenical work among Christians? What does it say about relations with the ELCA? interfaith work with Islam and Judaism? the worldwide Methodist/Wesleyan family?

The United Methodist Publishing House
www.umph.com
Cokesbury (no longer a local retailer, but still online at www.cokesbury.com)

What other denominations does Cokesbury serve? What challenges might this present, that is, potential confusion about what resources are really United Methodist?

General Commission on Religion and Race
www.gcorr.org

General Council on Finance and Administration
www.gcfa.org

An important and powerful agency. What does it do? How does it relate to your conference CFA and your church?

GENERAL BOARD OF
Higher Education
& Ministry

www.gbhem.org

How does thie agency relate to your conference Board of Ordained Ministry, District Committees on Ministry, and United Methodist seminaries? What seminary(ies) are you closest to in proximity? What does this organization offer for the ministry of the laity?

DISCIPLESHIP MINISTRIES
The United Methodist Church

www.gbod.org

This agency provides the Lay Servant Ministries program resources and materials. It also equips the church with numerous publications (among them are devotionals for children, youth, and adults). It is the headquarters of the ecumenical Walk to Emmaus program and the Academy for Spiritual Formation. What else do you find on the Discipleship Ministries website that might be helpful to both individuals and your local church?

UMM
UNITED METHODIST MEN

www.gcumm.org

What does United Methodist Men do to support youth programs and men's ministries? What else do UMM groups do? What resources does UMM have available for your church?

Global Ministries
The United Methodist Church

www.gbgm-umc.org

This is the main missionary-sending agency of The United Methodist Church. What does it do? Where can you find information about missionaries and missions? Today, most churches and church organizations have their own websites, but the GBGM website was a pioneer in hosting church websites, and it still offers this service free of charge.

General Board of Pension and Health Benefits of The United Methodist Church

www.gbophb.org

An important agency to your pastor. What does it do? How are its activities connected to concern for peace and justice in the world?

GCSRW
General Commission on the Status and Role of Women

www.gcsrw.org

What does this agency do? Are your annual conference sessions monitored by one of its representatives?

General Board of CHURCH & SOCIETY of The United Methodist Church

www.umc-gbcs.org

What does this agency do? How does it relate to your Conference Board of Church and Society? What resources does it have available for your church?

United Methodist Women
FAITH · HOPE · LOVE IN ACTION

new.gbgm-umc.org/umw/

No longer a division of GBGM but an independent organization, UMW continues its long tradition as a major supporter of missions focused on serving women and children around the world and as a major educator of United Methodists on world issues. Local units are now free to organize in new ways in support of this mission. What resources does it have available for your church? Does your conference UMW offer Schools of Mission?

UMCOR
United Methodist Committee On Relief

www.umcor.org

The United Methodist Committee on Relief is a source of great pride for United Methodists. How is it funded? What is the "Advance" and how much of Advance donations go to direct aid? Where does UMCOR operate? What are relief-supply kits? Where is your nearest UMCOR supply warehouse? How can churches participate directly in responding to disasters with money, supplies, and trained volunteers? What disaster response training is available in your conference?

Human Relations Day Offering

www.umcgiving.org/site/c.qwL6KkNWLrH/b.6817081/k.83AD/Human_Relations_Day_Sunday.htm

---

One Great Hour of Sharing (UMCOR)

www.umcgiving.org/site/c.qwL6KkNWLrH/b.6817113/k.3FCD/One_Great_Hour_of_Sharing_Sunday.htm

---

Native American Ministries Sunday

www.umcgiving.org/site/c.qwL6KkNWLrH/b.6839695/k.46E0/Native_American_Ministries_Sunday.htm

---

Peace with Justice Sunday

www.umcgiving.org/site/c.qwL6KkNWLrH/b.6839711/k.6336/Peace_with_Justice_Sunday.htm

---

World Communion Sunday

www.umcgiving.org/site/c.qwL6KkNWLrH/b.7080289/k.7AC8/World_Communion_Sunday.htm

---

United Methodist Student Day

www.umcgiving.org/site/c.qwL6KkNWLrH/b.7080529/k.EB25/United_Methodist_Student_Day.htm

---

> If your class is large enough, ask participants to select one of the following caucus groups to highlight the diversity of The United Methodist Church. (Note: the Marcha website is in Spanish.) These slips relate only to United States participants.

BLACK METHODISTS FOR CHURCH RENEWAL

www.bmcrumc.org

What resources does BMCR offer your church? Is there a BMCR unit in your conference?

Native American International Caucus
www.naicumc.org

What resources does NAIC offer your church? Is there an NAIC unit in your conference?

National Federation of Asian American United Methodists
www.nfaaum.org

What resources does NFAAUM offer your church? Is there an NFAAUM unit in your conference? (There is also a Pacific Islander National Caucus of United Methodists, but at this printing it has no website.)

MARCHA
Metodistas Asociados Representando
la Causa de los Hispano-Americanos

Methodists Associated Representing the Cause of Hispanic Americans
www.marchaumc.org

Is there a MARCHA unit in your conference? What resources does MARCHA offer Hispanic churches?

Note: Some class participants may be connected to one or more of a number of issue-oriented caucus groups related to The United Methodist Church. While there is no reason to address these in class, you should be familiar with them so that you can briefly answer questions, hopefully outside of the class sessions. A good summary and listing can be found on this website: www.umportal.org/article.asp?id=3160!

Session Five Discussion Topics

Select the topics you wish to use based on the number of participants in the class and the interests they have shown throughout the course. Print three or four copies of each topic so that everyone in the small group can have one. Or, have everyone (or more than one group) study the same topic. You can also create your own topics based on other interests shown by participants—for example:

- How are apportionments determined? What expenses (health insurance) are directly billed to churches? Is there a better way of financing?
- How does the Conference Board of Ordained Ministry process candidates for ministry?
- What commissions, committees, and task groups in your annual conference need lay members—specifically the missional gifts of class participants?
- How do candidates move through the "process" toward ordination? What is the local church's role in evaluating and assisting candidates?
- What are the benefits and drawbacks—to the clergyperson and the local church—of licensed local pastor status? elder? deacon?
- If your conference has just merged or may merge, what structural issues must be addressed? what practical issues? As conferences become larger geographically, how can technology keep them connected?

Groups should have access and refer to the latest version of the *Book of Discipline*. The references given here are from the 2008 edition. Encourage participants to use their tablets or smartphones, if possible, to access and search general church resources at http://www.umc.org, as well as the website for the Council of Bishops and Judicial Council. If you do not have access to the Internet, you may copy key parts of online resources, shown in the URLs for each topic, which you can then distribute to participants. Be familiar with the issues you choose so that you can answer questions and, if necessary, correct misconceptions. Encourage students to speak to one another in Christian love during their conversations.

Guaranteed Appointment and Itinerancy

Book of Discipline references
Restrictive Rules (¶19 and ¶20)
Ministry, Authority, and Responsibilities of an Elder in Full Connection (¶334)
Complaint Procedures (¶361)

The 2012 General Conference saw an effort from the Study of Ministry Commission to end "security of appointment," more generally known as "guaranteed appointment." General Conference approved the proposal on the consent calendar without debate and an effort to reconsider failed. This legislation would have permitted bishops to appoint elders to less than full-time positions on their own initiative and, with the approval of the annual conference clergy session, place elders on unpaid "transitional leave" for up to twenty-four months.

General Conference also asked the Judicial Council for a declaratory decision about this move, and in Decision 1226, the council ruled it unconstitutional, stating:

> Security of appointment has long been a part of the tradition of The United Methodist Church and its predecessor bodies. Abolishing security of appointment would destroy our historic plan for our itinerant superintendency. Fair process procedures, trials and appeals are integral parts of the privilege of our clergy of right to trial by a committee and of appeal and is an absolute right which cannot be eradicated by legislation. . . .
>
> We have found no instance in which there have been provisions for not appointing clergy involuntarily to ministerial settings other than chargeable offenses or some form of unacceptability for appointment (http://archives.umc.org/interior_judicial.asp?mid=263&JDID=1340&JDMOD=VWD).

The legislation was ruled to be in violation of the third and fourth Restrictive Rules (¶19 and ¶20). The security of appointment principle was first written in the 1956 *Discipline* and was maintained in the 1968 merger. However, the Judicial Council ruling did not address new legislation that gave the bishop and the cabinet the right to initiate a part-time appointment. The General Board of Higher Education and Ministry points out that such a move should not be used for punishment or remedial action against a clergyperson. For information about the part-time legislation and the existing process to deal with ineffective clergy, see http://www.pnwumc.org/news/gbhem-recommends-care-with-use-of-part-time-appointment/.

Discuss: *What is your take on this issue? What are the benefits of guaranteed appointment? What are the drawbacks? What are the measures of effectiveness for clergy in the twenty-first century? Given this Judicial Council ruling, how could the procedures for dealing with ineffectiveness be streamlined? should they?*

Sexual Orientation

Book of Discipline references
Unauthorized Conduct (¶341.6)
Qualifications for Ordination (¶304.2-3) and *Candidacy for Licensed and Ordained Ministry* (¶311.2d) Chargeable Offenses and the Statute of Limitations (¶2702)
Social Principles (¶161 B, F, and ¶162 J)
Judicial Council decisions 702, 722, 725, and 984

In the same issue of the *United Methodist Reporter* that published Reverend Christy Krum's blog on November 30, 2012, stating that the polity of The United Methodist Church is broken beyond repair, retired Bishop Woodie White spoke of the time when he, as a young pastor, and two other African American clergy met with the pastor of a white church in the South to let him know that they intended to visit his church the next day, even though the church had voted against permitting black persons to worship there. Reverend White then pointed to the paragraphs in the 1960 *Discipline*, "The Methodist Social Creed," that said:

> "[T]he right to . . . join a church should not be limited by a person's race. . . ." [The pastor] quietly but emphatically said, "None of that is the law of the Church." He stated that neither the Social Creed nor Resolutions are the law of the Methodist Church and he did not have to follow either. . . . I recovered, and said, "You mean if it were the law of the church, you would follow it? . . ." He responded, "Of course, I'm a Methodist!"
>
> United Methodism has a self-correcting polity. Every four years we open the *Book of Discipline* and seek to state in it what we believe is the best and clearest expression of Christ in contemporary society. Sometimes we get it right. And sometimes, many believe, we get it wrong. . . .

Sexual orientation is not the only issue causing strain within The United Methodist Church in the twenty-first century, but it is perhaps one of the more emotional issues. For some, the church has gotten it right around the issue. For others, the issue remains an example of how the church has gotten it wrong.

An historical overview of the church's struggle with the issue of sexual orientation can be found at www.umc.org/site/c.lwL4KnN1LtH/b.4074843/k.6C9C/Homosexuality_Overview.htm. As the webpage notes, the issue was first inserted into the Social Principles in 1972. Like the Social Creed (now a short statement that does not mention race), the Social Principles were not considered church law, though they are now listed in ¶311.2.d as requirements for clergy candidates (generally only the homosexuality clause is used now to disqualify candidates).

American society was also struggling with the issue of homosexuality during this time. In 1973, the board of the American Psychiatric Association removed homosexuality from its *Diagnostic and Statistical Manual of Mental Disorders.* Since then, United Methodists on opposite sides of the issue, backed by unofficial caucuses, have been attending General Conference and the arguments surrounding the issue have increased in bitterness. Meanwhile, societal attitudes on homosexuality in the United States are changing as more states vote to legalize same-sex marriage. While African conferences, conferences in the Southeastern Jurisdiction, and the Philippines are seen as primarily opposed to changes in the "incompatibility" language, and United Methodists in the Northeastern, North Central, and Western Jurisdictions are seen as primarily in favor of it, the fact remains that opinion is not uniform in any of these geographical areas. We do not agree.

In response, the Western Jurisdiction has adopted a "Statement of Gospel Obedience" calling for bishops and clergy to "operate as if the statement in ¶161 F does not exist, creating a church in which all people are truly welcome." (See www.pnwumc.org/news/what-does-a-statement-of-gospel-obedience-mean-for-the-church/.)

Others have noted that in various conferences, The United Methodist Church does in fact include gay and lesbian clergy, and even partnered gay and lesbian clergy. The unofficial Reconciling Ministries Network now includes hundreds of churches that are open to and affirming of gay and lesbian members (a stance that is not technically illegal under the *Discipline*) and hundreds of clergy who have signed a pledge stating they are available to officiate same-sex marriages. Many younger members—and former members—of The United Methodist Church are no longer willing to live under what amounts to "don't ask, don't tell."

Discuss: *Study the disciplinary references listed above. If you would like to learn more, check out the Judicial Council decisions. What does this controversy mean for* *the churches in your conference and your own local church? What might happen to the church if bishops and churches in the Western Jurisdiction obey their "Statement of Gospel Obedience?" Is there a way for the church to make room to "agree to disagree" on this issue? How might this work?*

General Conference in a Global Church

Book of Discipline references
General Conference (¶8 and ¶¶13–16)
Central Conferences (¶¶540–548)

General Conference is eleven days of nonstop, sleep-deprived stress and great expense for the nearly one thousand delegates who are elected to attend. Some of the stress relates to the fact that General Conference spends significant time on details of administration that pertain only to the United States, such as clergy pensions. Delegates from the central conferences (outside the United States) have little interest in such proceedings, but they must wade through them anyway and vote on all matters in the *Book of Discipline*. The central conferences do have the authority to change the *Book of Discipline* to meet local cultural needs (¶543.7–21). Clergy and laypeople in the United States, especially those concerned with the church's stance on homosexuality, question why American United Methodists cannot do the same.

An issue in recent decades has been—and will likely continue to be—the way in which The United Methodist Church can be a global church and still connect with local cultures, including those in the United States. The global connection of The United Methodist Church has accomplished great and amazing work in spreading the gospel and building the kingdom. But in an age of growing decentralization of power, what does it mean to be a global church centered in the United States? On the other hand, in an age that is also witnessing the globalization of communication, information, and commerce, what does it mean to be a global church that only meets once every four years?

Discuss: *How useful is General Conference and the global connection as it is currently structured? What if General Conference met outside the United States—for example, Africa? What advantages and disadvantages might there be to this? What responsibilities does The United Methodist Church in the United States have for the salaries and pensions of clergy outside the United States? To what extent does the economic inequality among areas of the church contribute to certain stresses within the church? Do you think the global church should be restructured for the twenty-first century? If so, how?*

The Cost of Doing Business with the General Agencies

Book of Discipline references
¶16.9, ¶47, ¶701–710
Judicial Council decision 1210

At the 2012 General Conference, three reorganization plans for The United Methodist Church were voted down. A fourth plan was ultimately passed, Plan UMC, and it was immediately declared unconstitutional by the Judicial Council. You can find the decision here: http://archives.umc.org/interior_judicial.asp?mid=263&JDID=1331&JDMOD=VWD&SN=1201&EN=1230.

There is no need to go into detail about Plan UMC or its predecessors. The point is that all of the plans were efforts to save money by streamlining the general church boards and agencies, making them smaller and more nimble and giving them more budgeting power. Plan UMC provided for a General Council for Strategy and Oversight that would oversee all program agencies and centralize administrative services.

While efficiency, smaller size, and nimbleness are valuable in any organization, opponents pointed out that reducing the size of the boards and agencies would also reduce the diversity of their membership. The Judicial Council ruled that the Constitution places general oversight in the Council of Bishops, and thus Plan UMC violated ¶47 and ¶705.5d. They also determined that the plan violated the Constitution ¶16.9 which authorizes only General Conference to "determine and provide for raising and distributing funds necessary to carry on the work of the Church."

Discuss: *Does the structure of the general church agencies need to be reorganized? If so, in view of the constitutional strictures about oversight and finance, what might this reorganization look like? If not, what values does our current structure support? Is there any way to make our structures more efficient—that is, less costly—within the parameters of the Constitution?*

The Trust Clause and Local Church Property Issues

Book of Discipline references
Church Property and Trust Clauses (¶¶2501–2503)
Local Church Property (¶¶2524–2550)

The Trust Clause has been upheld by the American court system many times. Note that the trust clause language does not need to be present in a deed for it to have effect. A church is deemed to be a United Methodist Church covered by the trust clause if it has looked United Methodist, acted United Methodist, called itself United Methodist, or received a United Methodist pastor (¶2503.6).

Church property from discontinued congregations is cared for by the annual conference Board of Trustees until the property can be sold or conveyed to a new congregation, either United Methodist or from a denomination represented in the Commission on Pan-Methodist Cooperation and Union (¶2548). If property is sold, it is used as the annual conference sees fit. In many conferences, the proceeds from sales of closed churches are held specifically for the purpose of planting new churches.

The Conference Board of Trustees also manages intangible property from closed churches, such as endowment assets.

On the other end of the church life cycle, congregations do not move or spin off daughter congregations on their own, but only in cooperation with the district superintendent and District Board of Church Location and Building, also known as the district site committee (¶ 2519). The goal of this is to ensure that churches have good sites with adequate land and are located in places where there is likely to be a sufficient population to sustain them. Sometimes congregations look at such requirements as another hoop they have to jump through, but these requirements are helpful in the process of expanding existing churches and planting new ones. Also, there are often resource persons available to consult with churches and offer suggestions for the better use of existing space. Inquire about what help is available from your district and conference.

Discuss: *What issues around church property might arise in the twenty-first century? As house churches become more common and congregations begin meeting exclusively online, will church buildings become something of the past? What are the benefits of a local church owning property? What are the drawbacks? It is sometimes said—in seriousness more or less—that the clergy pension plan and the trust clause is the glue that holds The United Methodist Church together in the face of the stresses and strains of the changing world, simply because it would be too expensive for clergy and congregations to leave The United Methodist Church. What do you think about this statement? How are United Methodist congregations learning to be diverse within the connection? What are the benefits of the trust clause? What are the drawbacks?*

Bivocational Clergy

Book of Discipline references
Qualifications for Ordination (¶304.1d)
The Itinerant System (¶338)

The itinerancy system has traditionally depended on elders and full-time local pastors appointed to full-time charges who are compensated according to the conference equitable salary structure for full-time work. In fact, full-time work is part of elder and deacon candidates' own covenant vows. The full-time rule means a smaller membership church may share a pastor with one or more churches, some of which may be geographically distant from the others. This can cause stress and resentment. Sometimes churches cannot even afford to pay the pastor a quarter-time salary.

Because of the connection, however, conferences can find ways to provide pastoral leadership to small membership churches and church plants. Often this is by a part-time local pastor or student local pastor. Sometimes a student, local pastor, deacon, certified lay minister, or lay speaker on staff (paid or volunteer) in a stronger church is "lent" to the smaller church. Particularly in the Hispanic community, lay missioners, who make their living outside the church, are trained and appointed to start new Spanish-language congregations.

Deacons, whose primary appointment is beyond the local church, must have a secondary appointment in a charge conference. This requirement has led some churches to think of deacons as full-time staff members without pay, even if they are employed full-time elsewhere. And sometimes, since deacons do not *have* to be paid, they *do* serve as volunteer staff while looking for work or working part-time.

Before the 2012 General Conference, ¶338 made it clear that elders could be appointed to less than full-time service, but only *at the request* of the elder (and the approval of the clergy session). The 2012 legislation on itinerancy authorized bishops and their cabinets to appoint an elder to less than full-time service *without* the elder's request. Although the Judicial Council struck down the "end of guaranteed appointment" features of the legislation, the part-time appointment feature was left intact. In all of these ways, pastoral leadership for small- and medium-sized membership churches is moving toward including what are traditionally called "tent-making" ministries, named after the apostle Paul and the way in which he earned his living while founding a church.

Discuss: *What are the benefits to "tent-making" (bivocational) ministries, both for the church and for the clergyperson? What are the drawbacks? Are there missional benefits besides church finances? How has your conference worked to ensure that every local church has pastoral leadership? Do you expect bivocational clergy to become more common in the future?*

Printed in the USA
CPSIA information can be obtained
at www.ICGtesting.com
JSHW010901130224
57185JS00007B/15

9 780881 777017